Contents

- 4 Introduction
- 5 The Moth
- 6 The Judge
- 7 The Tap
- 8 The Child's Homework
- 9 The Charity Collector
- 10 The Magnifying Glass
- 11 The Film Critic
- 12 The Loose Change
- 13 The Hot Shower
- 14 The Excavation
- 15 The Fast-Food Restaurant
- 16 The Muslim
- 17 The Loose Connection
- 18 The Credit Card Statement
- 19 The Hall of Mirrors
- 20 The Quality Control Stamp
- 21 The Phone Call
- 22 The Carnival
- 23 The Door
- 24 The Curtains
- 25 The Burst Pipe
- 26 The Binoculars
- 27 The Protest March
- 28 The Knotted Hankie
- 29 The Frown
- 30 The Parrot
- 31 The Child's Confession
- 32 The Whitewash

Introduction

The promise of God's unfailing mercy has inspired generations of Christians across the years, but though they may be confident of his willingness to forgive, many still struggle when it comes to acknowledging their faults. Where should they start, what words should they use, and what exactly do they have to confess? Too often they end up repeating well-worn ideas or petering out before they've barely begun, all of which can create a sense of frustration if not failure.

If that's been your experience, don't despair, for perhaps the problem lies simply in the way you approach such prayer. Our tendency is to shut the world out in our attempt to focus on God, yet that risks divorcing faith from daily life, almost as though the two are mutually exclusive. Such a dichotomy is entirely misplaced, for true belief should touch every aspect of who and what we are—the good as much as the bad. Time and again I've found God speaking through the world around me, not only bringing his challenge but also evoking a response. Ordinary experiences can help us express ourselves in "ordinary" language, speaking both of our mistakes and of his mercy.

The prayers in this book, drawn from four of my recent publications, reflect everyday moments that led me to acknowledge particular faults while at the same time celebrating God's forgiveness. Each pointed beyond itself, inspiring repentance and renewal. I offer them in the hope that God may speak similarly to you.

Nick Fawcett

The Moth

It fluttered around the flame,
inexorably drawn—
surely sensing the danger
yet unable to resist—
and it was only a matter of time
before its wings were scorched
and the hapless creature fell.

Like the moth, Lord, I am attracted by what deceives,
promising life yet delivering death.
I try to fight it,
aware of the danger,
but the lure is too strong;
all sense forgotten when temptation strikes.
Draw me close to you
and shine in my darkness,
bringing the light that leads to life.
Amen.

The Judge

It was his job to pass sentence.
Whatever his feelings on the matter,
his duty was clear:
not to show mercy
but to deliver a punishment that fit the crime.

You, Lord, have cause to punish,
more grounds for passing sentence than any,
for I repeatedly flout your will
and disobey your commandments,
but your nature is always to pardon.
Instead of holding my faults against me,
you offer full and free forgiveness,
the opportunity to start again.
For the wonder of your mercy,
Lord, I thank you.
Amen.

The Tap

I turn on the tap,
and there it is,
water when and where I want it—
to wash the dishes,
water the garden,
take a bath,
have a drink,
and so much else besides—
enough, and more than enough, for all my needs.

Forgive me, Lord,
for I treat *you* like a tap sometimes,
expecting you to supply whatever I want,
whenever I want it—
blessings on demand.
Remind me that you *do* provide—
more than I can ever ask for—
but not necessarily the things of this world,
your gifts being of a different kind,
nurturing the spirit and enriching within.
Teach me to thirst for such things—
gifts of your kingdom—
and to be truly satisfied.
Amen.

The Child's Homework

He knew he had to do it
but he kept on putting it off,
postponing the evil moment.
And finally, when he could delay it no longer,
he raced to get it finished—
the attempt desultory,
as little as he could get away with.

Forgive me, Lord, for I'm careless in discipleship,
reluctant to move away from the comfort zone.
Forgive the complacency of my commitment,
my doing as little rather than as much as possible,
and teach me to offer instead not what I *must*
but what I *may* do in your service,
in glad and joyful response.
Amen.

The Charity Collector

They were there outside the supermarket,
shaking their tins hopefully,
but I averted my eyes and shuffled past,
pretending I hadn't noticed their presence.
I'd no loose change to salve my conscience—
just a five-dollar bill, nothing smaller—
so I hurried by on the other side.

Lord, forgive me,
for I'd spent more on one treat for myself
than the five dollars I begrudged to others.
I'd extolled the virtue of a generous heart
yet displayed the meanest of spirits,
my talk of concern and compassion
exposed for the sham it was.
Teach me, next time I'm asked to give,
to respond gladly,
and to offer not the least I can get away with
but more than I can truly afford.
Amen.

The Magnifying Glass

I was scared for a moment,
for there among the blades of grass
were monstrosities—
hideous and terrifying,
like nothing I'd seen before.
Yet, of course, they were just ordinary insects—
ants, beetles, and the like,
magnified beyond recognition.

Forgive me, Lord,
for I make a similar mistake in life,
repeatedly magnifying things out of all proportion.
I turn minor weaknesses into major faults,
disappointments into tragedies,
and problems into crises;
trivial disputes blown up into blazing fights
and innocent remarks taken as personal slights.
Help me to gain a balanced perspective,
with your help seeing things as they really are.
Amen.

The Film Critic

She tore it to pieces,
panning the plot, dialogue, effects, and acting,
nothing and no one escaping her attack—
the film, in her view, not simply a disaster movie
but a disaster through and through.
Was she right?
Who can say?
But, of course, it was her job to pick holes,
even if she took it to excess,
her role as a critic being on the line.

I, Lord, find fault for less reason,
all too swift to condemn and slow to praise.
I focus on weaknesses rather than strengths,
faults instead of virtues,
failure instead of success;
the negatives swamping the positives
until I can see nothing else.
Forgive me,
and instead of dwelling on the worst in people,
help me to see the best.
Amen.

The Loose Change

I pocketed the coins with barely a glance,
the sum so small it seemed hardly worth counting;
yet what *I* judged insignificant
others would have considered a fortune,
enough to spell the difference between life and death.
It could have bought food for the hungry,
medicine for the sick,
or shelter for the homeless;
but it did none of those,
lying instead in my pocket
until spent, not on others, but myself.

Forgive me, Lord,
for I have received so much yet give so little,
frittering away money
on trivia and luxuries I do not need,
while a multitude suffer and die for want of a pittance.
Remind me of how fortunate I am
and of all I can do for others at such minimal cost,
and teach me to respond,
ready to give not just my small change, but
sacrificially,
just as you gave your all for me.
Amen.

The Hot Shower

I washed gratefully,
rinsing away the dirt, dust, sweat, and smoke,
the grittiness from my eyes
and weariness from my limbs,
and I felt not just refreshed but clean,
almost made new.

Lord, with you there's no *almost* about it:
you wash us from within,
cleansing the thoughts of the heart,
transforming and restoring,
offering a fresh start,
new beginnings,
day after day.
Wash me, I pray, in the fountain of your love.
Amen.

The Excavation

Who would have thought it?—
so special a find,
so rare an artifact,
hidden so near
for so long—
a nondescript patch of earth yielding hidden treasure.

Forgive me, Lord,
for I judge people by what I see,
too often failing to delve deeper,
and, in consequence, I miss hidden gems,
the pearl within the oyster.
Teach me never to dismiss anyone,
however ordinary they may seem.
Open my heart instead to the value in all.
Amen.

The Fast-Food Restaurant

There was no shortage of customers:
morning, afternoon, and evening
they piled through the doors,
the mountain of debris they left behind
testimony to their appetite.
And why not,
for it was cheap, tasty, and convenient,
though as for nutrition,
best not to ask.

I'm good at filling my body, Lord,
if careless sometimes what I eat,
but when it comes to my soul it's a sorrier tale.
Turning my back on food that satisfies—
living bread,
true sustenance—
I cram it instead with junk food,
a diet that, instead of nourishing, undermines health,
leaving me spiritually flabby,
inwardly weak.
Forgive me,
and teach me to feast at your table
instead of snacking on empty morsels.
Amen.

The Muslim

He sat in the subway car,
aware of the eyes turned on him—
inquisitive eyes, intrigued by his appearance,
suspicious eyes, fearful of some hidden agenda,
hostile eyes, resentful at his presence—
so many eyes failing to see behind the labels
or below the surface
to the person underneath.

Forgive me, Lord, for the way I too pigeonhole people,
unconsciously absorbing the prejudices of society even
as I resist them,
shaped by fears and preconceptions
I'm barely aware of,
hiding behind generalizations that say more about me
than others.
Open my eyes to see people as they are,
rather than as I construe them to be.
Amen.

The Loose Connection

It was just a loose wire, that's all,
nothing major,
but though everything else was in perfect order,
that faulty connection spelled problems,
impeding the flow of current until it was fixed.

Lord, it's the same with me, I'm afraid—
your Spirit's power is too often prevented
from getting through.
I don't mean it to happen,
and don't willfully go wrong;
it's just that I allow little things,
small distractions,
to come between us,
inexorably multiplying,
until I become detached from you,
all contact broken,
and the flow is stopped.
Forgive me, Lord,
restore the circuit,
and connect me again.
Amen.

The Credit Card Statement

It was there in black and white,
chilling,
inescapable.
He'd spent more than he realized,
more than he could afford,
and was left now with a debt around his neck,
an amount owing that would take months,
even years,
to repay.

Lord, I can never earn your love,
still less repay your goodness toward me,
but you do not ask me to.
You have cancelled the debt,
writing it off as though it had never been.
Though I owe so much,
you ask me simply to receive.
Though I deserve so little,
you offer new life in Christ,
free and overflowing.
For the awesome generosity of your gift,
Lord, I thank you.
Amen.

The Hall of Mirrors

We laughed together,
for the images were grotesque,
hideously distorted—
our legs like matchsticks,
chests like tree trunks,
faces stretched and figures squashed
beyond recognition—
a travesty of the truth.
It was funny because it was phoney,
each reflection an intended caricature,
a distortion of reality.

What do people see in me, Lord,
beneath the mask of piety
and veneer of commitment?
What picture do I give them?
What image convey of you?
Forgive me,
for I see now, in a rare moment of honesty,
the false and flawed reflection I offer,
and I'm laughing no longer,
for it's another caricature,
as gross as the other,
only this time there's no mirror;
it's all too real.
Amen.

The Quality Control Stamp

It had been rigorously tested,
checked and checked again,
declared fit for use
only after it had met exacting criteria,
the standards required by quality control.

How would I fare, Lord, were I to be similarly checked,
my life scrutinized,
assessed,
weighed in the balance?
Would I come up to scratch,
pass muster as a follower of Christ?
I fear not,
for there's so much wrong in my life,
so many ways I fall short.
Yet the mystery is that you *do* examine me,
searching my heart and weighing the spirit,
and though I fail on innumerable counts,
still you accept me as I am,
enough to call me your child.
For that awesome, astonishing truth,
Lord, I thank you.
Amen.

The Phone Call

She put me on hold with the usual platitudes—
"Won't be a moment" . . .
"Your call will be dealt with" . . .
"Thank you for waiting"—
and half an hour later I was *still* waiting,
still listening to the infuriating jingle
and occasional recorded message,
apparently forgotten in the queue.

Forgive me, Lord,
for, time after time, I put *you* on hold,
making time for you when it suits me
but then turning to other things,
forgetting you are even there.
Whatever I'm doing,
wherever I am,
help me stay connected—
ready to listen to your voice
and respond.
Amen.

The Carnival

A carnival atmosphere, they called it . . .
and it was—
people dancing and singing in the streets,
laughing, applauding, chatting, and cheering,
everywhere a sea of exuberant celebration.
For one day, at least,
the drabness of life was swept away,
replaced by a vibrant tapestry of sound and color.

Lord, I have so much to celebrate,
yet instead of rejoicing in all you have given,
the countless blessings you so freely shower upon me,
I brood over disappointments,
fret about the future,
complain about my lot,
and dwell on my troubles
until I can no longer see beyond them,
my spirit closed to the generosity of your provision.
Forgive me,
and teach me each day
to exult in your awesome gift of life,
now and for all eternity.
Amen.

The Door

He knocked and knocked again,
but there was no answer,
the door being firmly closed,
denying entry.
Was there no one at home?
Were his knocks unheard?
Or was his presence ignored,
his company unwelcome?

Lord,
forgive me for closing the door to you,
repeatedly denying you access into my life.
Forgive me for shutting you out
when your presence unsettles
and your word confronts,
when you ask questions of me I would rather not face
and make demands I prefer to avoid.
Open my heart to your love,
my mind to your truth,
and my soul to your grace,
so that you might live in me
and I in you.
Amen.

The Curtains

The sun was too bright,
pouring in through the window,
so I closed the curtains
until the light dimmed
and I could open them once more.
But when it grew dark,
I closed them again,
this time keeping light *in* lest prying eyes intrude.

Forgive me, Lord,
for I do much the same with *your* light,
stopping it from shining either *in* or *out*.
Pull back the curtains I close against you,
so that the light of your love
and radiance of your presence
may flood into my heart
and out through my life.
Amen.

The Burst Pipe

It didn't look much,
just a small hole in the pipe,
but water gushed from it—
through the ceiling,
down the walls,
and across the floor—
leaving the room sodden,
décor ruined.

Lord, my faults seem small,
barely worth bothering with sometimes,
yet the consequences can be greater than I expect,
an apparently trivial mistake
having potentially devastating repercussions.
However minor my weaknesses may be,
teach me to consider where they might lead
and to put things right
before lasting damage is done.
Amen.

The Binoculars

I couldn't see *everything*,
not by a long shot,
but I could see more than before—
much more—
details previously hidden from view
suddenly revealed,
blurred images brought sharply into focus,
opening up new horizons,
possibilities I never even knew existed.

Lord, when it comes to you
and the things of your kingdom,
I glimpse only the vaguest outline of reality,
a mere fraction of the truth,
yet I confuse this partial picture with the full vista,
imagining I have seen all I need to see.
Forgive me,
and open my eyes to the wonder of your presence,
the fullness of your truth,
the richness of your love,
and the immensity of your purpose.
Amen.

The Protest March

They lined the streets,
hundreds of thousands of them,
banners waving
like some mighty army going into battle
as they marched on the city,
but they brandished words, not weapons,
their fight being for justice,
freedom,
hope,
and truth.

Forgive me, Lord,
for though I see evil, I keep quiet,
afraid to speak out
or too lazy to take a stand.
For all my talk of lofty ideals
I rarely have the courage of my convictions,
leaving it instead to others
to expose wrongdoing and tackle injustice.
Teach me not simply to espouse principles in private
but to uphold and defend them,
my allegiance plain to all.
Amen.

The Knotted Hankie

It was there to remind me, that much was obvious,
but to remind me of what was less clear.
I'd tried various tricks to jog the memory,
but each to no avail,
time and again forgetting vital details,
special dates,
or important engagements,
my mind a blank when I needed to remember most.

Forgive me, Lord, for I forget *you* just as easily,
your many gifts and countless promises
slipping from my mind.
Slow to recall your faithfulness across the years,
I fail to make time for you as I should,
overlooking your awesome goodness
and taking your love for granted.
Remind me of all you are,
all you have done,
and all you are doing,
and keep such knowledge fresh in my mind,
each moment of every day.
Amen.

The Frown

It made me uneasy, that look on his face,
feeling that I'd done something wrong,
somehow displeased him.
But I'd misunderstood entirely,
his frown one of concentration rather than anger,
and my discomfort in his presence
altogether misplaced.

Too easily, Lord,
I picture *you* with a frown on your face—
stern,
forbidding,
angry—
as though you are permanently displeased
at my behavior,
looking for the opportunity to step in and condemn.
Remind me that the reality is so very different,
your nature being always to have mercy,
to forgive, love, and accept.
Help me, then, this and every day,
to celebrate your love
that smiles so constantly upon me.
Amen.

The Parrot

It sounded good—
an accomplished repertoire for a *person*,
let alone a *parrot*!
Only, of course, I wasn't fooled,
for though it seemed to speak,
made all the right noises,
it did so mechanically,
simply repeating what it had heard,
with no idea of the meaning,
the sense behind the words.

Forgive me, Lord,
for so much of my faith is parroted—
imitation commitment,
pastiche discipleship—
sounding impressive,
looking the part,
yet in reality borrowed from others,
echoing their experiences,
using their language,
repeating the established jargon,
without truly speaking *to* and *for* me.
Draw me close to you each day
in a deep and vibrant relationship,
so that what I say with my lips
I may truly believe in my heart.
Amen.

The Child's Confession

I could see that he was worried,
troubled by something deep inside,
but I couldn't work out what,
being forced instead to stand by helplessly
as he wrestled with his demons.
But then, finally, he plucked up courage
and blurted it out,
confessing to his little "crime" —
small in *my* eyes
but huge in *his*.
There were tears then,
first of sorrow
but then relief,
as he realized it was dealt with,
finished
and forgiven.

Teach me, Lord, to confess my sins to you
instead of struggling with guilt
or hiding away in fear;
to let go of the burden,
knowing that you seek to pardon
rather than condemn,
bless instead of punish.
Help me, then,
openly and honestly to acknowledge my faults,
so that I may find the freedom you alone can give.
Amen.

The Whitewash

It was basic, true,
plain to the point of stark,
but it did the job,
covering a multitude of sins—
cracks, hollows, stains, and mold all neatly hidden—
but, of course, it was no real answer,
the problems merely being masked rather than tackled,
and it would be only a matter of time
before they surfaced again,
as bad as they were before.

There are as many faults in my life, Lord,
and I try the same trick,
attempting to whitewash over them,
hide them from view.
But only *you* can do that,
your love covering what I can never hope to conceal.
Come now,
and though my sins are as scarlet,
make me whiter than snow.
Amen.

www.ingramcontent.com/pod-product-compliance
Lightning Source LLC
Chambersburg PA
CBHW052038070526
44584CB00020B/3152